ANIMAL ABILITIES

ELEPHANTS

Charlotte Guillain

Raintree is an imprint of Capstone Global Library Limited, a company incorporated in England and Wales having its registered office at 7 Pilgrim Street, London, EC4V 6LB – Registered company number: 6695582

www.raintreepublishers.co.uk
myorders@raintreepublishers.co.uk

Edited by Laura Knowles, Abby Colich, and Diyan Leake
Designed by Victoria Allen and Ken Vail Graphic Design
Original illustrations © Capstone Global Library Ltd 2013
Illustrated by HL Studios
Picture research by Elizabeth Alexander
Originated by Capstone Global Library Ltd
Printed and bound in China by CTPS

ISBN 978 1 406 25910 0 (hardback)
17 16 15 14 13
10 9 8 7 6 5 4 3 2 1

ISBN 978 1 406 25917 9 (paperback)
18 17 16 15 14
10 9 8 7 6 5 4 3 2 1

British Library Cataloguing in Publication Data
Guillain, Charlotte.
  Elephants. -- (Animal abilities)
  1. Elephants--Juvenile literature. 2. Animal intelligence--Juvenile literature.
  I. Title II. Series
  599.6'7-dc23

Acknowledgements
We would like to thank the following for permission to reproduce photographs: Getty Images pp. 8 (Johnny Haglund/Lonely Planet Images), 22 (Andrew Watson/Photolibrary); Nature Picture Library pp. 6 (© Jabruson), 19 (© Simon King); © Joshua Plotnik p. 13; Reuters p. 26 (Michaela Rehle); Shutterstock pp. 5 top (© Graeme Shannon), 10 (© Cucumber Images), 11 top (© Hedrus), 12 (© Johan Swanepoel), 15 (© LauraElizabeth), 17 (© Poulsons Photography), 18 (© Four Oaks), 20 (© Beat Glauser), 24 (© Francois van Heerden), 28 (© Lyubov Timofeyeva), 29 (© Aleksandar Todorovic); SuperStock pp. 5 bottom (© imagebroker.net), 7 (© imagebroker.net), 9 (© imagebroker.net), 14 (© age fotostock), 16 (© Juniors), 21 (© Minden Pictures), 23 (© LatitudeStock), 25 (© Robert Harding Picture Library), 27 (© Phanie). Design feature of an elephant silhoutte reproduced with permission of Shutterstock (© Tristan Tan).

Cover photograph of an African elephant reproduced with permission of Shutterstock (© Richard Peterson).

Contents

Some words are shown in bold, **like this**. You can find out what they mean by looking in the glossary.

Meet the elephants

The elephant is one of the most incredible animals on Earth. It is the largest animal living on land, and the second tallest after the giraffe. Elephants' long trunks, large, flat ears, pointed tusks, and thick, wrinkled, grey skin, make them unique. These strong, powerful animals are also very intelligent. They can push over trees, but can be extremely gentle and caring.

This map shows where different types of elephant live.

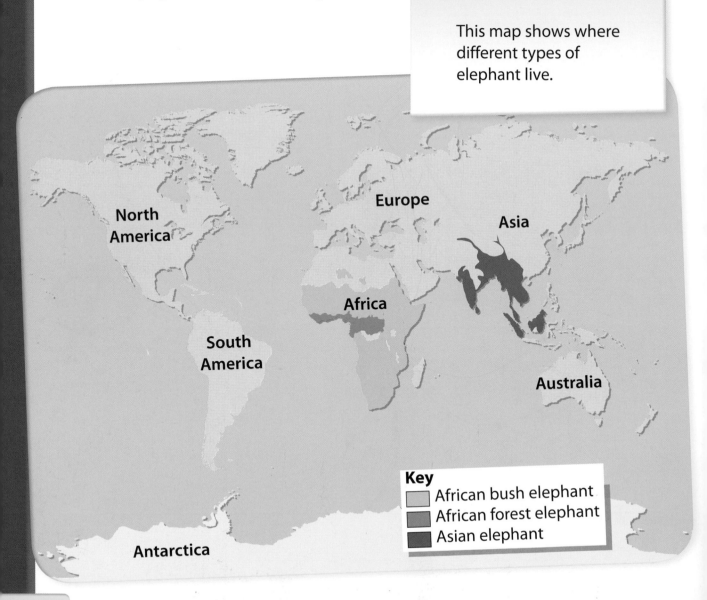

North America

Europe

Asia

Africa

South America

Australia

Antarctica

Key
- African bush elephant
- African forest elephant
- Asian elephant

There are three different **species** of elephant: the African bush elephant, the African forest elephant, and the Asian elephant. African bush elephants are the largest – they can weigh 8,000 kilograms (9 tons) and be 4 metres (13 feet) tall. African forest elephants are slightly smaller, with straighter tusks and more rounded ears. Asian elephants weigh about 5,500 kilograms (6 tons), can be around 3.5 metres (11½ feet) tall, and have much smaller ears than African elephants.

African bush elephants (right) have long tusks. Asian elephants (below) may have small tusks or no tusks at all.

Being an elephant

Elephants live in groups called herds. The different species of elephant live in different **habitats**. For example, African bush elephants mostly live on grassy plains called the **savannah**, but some live in deserts or swamps. African forest elephants live in rainforests in central and west Africa. Asian elephants live in forests in south and south-east Asia, in countries such as India, China, Indonesia, Sri Lanka, and Thailand.

This herd of African forest elephants is in the Odzala National Park in the Congo.

Daily life

Herds of elephants move around during the day, looking for food. Elephants eat grass, leaves, branches, roots, and fruits. They need to eat huge amounts every day to get the energy they need, and they will often spend around 16 hours a day feeding! Elephants will walk a long way to find water, which they use for drinking and bathing.

BIG FEEDERS

A wild elephant can eat 140 kilograms (300 pounds) of food in a day.

An elephant can drink 150 litres (40 gallons) of water a day.

Talented trunks

One of the elephant's most incredible features is its trunk. The trunk is in fact an extended top lip and nose. It is incredibly strong and flexible.

This elephant is using its trunk to breathe as it swims under water.

Like other animal noses, the trunk is used for breathing and smelling things. Elephants also use their trunk to drink – they suck water into it and then squirt it into their mouths. The trunk is also an important tool for feeding. An elephant uses its trunk to pull down tree branches and to carry food.

TERRIFIC TRUNK

There are no bones in an elephant's trunk. It can be 1.5 metres (5 feet) long and contains thousands of muscles.

African elephants have two sensitive, finger-like parts on the tip of their trunk. Asian elephants have one of these. They use these parts to pick up very small objects and they can carry very delicate items without breaking them.

Elephants can use the tip of their trunk to pick things up, similar to the way we use our fingers.

Using tools

One sign of an elephant's intelligence is the way it will use tools to solve problems. An elephant with an itch will pick up a branch with its trunk and use it to scratch an out-of-reach place.

Keeping cool

Living on the African savannah or in the rainforests of Asia, elephants can get very hot. Their large bodies also produce a lot of heat as they move around. Unlike many other **mammals**, elephants can't sweat to cool down. They are able to lower their body temperature in other ways.

THICK-SKINNED

An African elephant's skin can be 4 centimetres (2½ inches) thick on some parts of its body.

Beating the heat

Water and mud are very important for keeping elephants cool. They need to find rivers or waterholes to bathe in when they become hot. Elephants often cover themselves with mud to keep biting insects off their skin and stop the Sun burning them.

Elephants spray themselves with water to stay cool.

African elephants' ears help keep them cool.

An elephant's large ears play an important part in keeping the animal cool. The flat ears contain **blood vessels**. When the elephant's blood passes through the ears, it comes close to the surface of the skin and the heat in its blood can escape to the air around it. Elephants flap their ears to help this happen, because many of the blood vessels are on the back of their ears, where their skin is thinner.

heat leaving the elephant's body

elephant's ear

Elephants need their large ears to help them lose heat.

blood vessels

Elephant teamwork

Elephants are very **social** animals. They live in herds because they often work as a team. They help each other to find food and water, look after each other when they are injured or sick, and protect all the herd members from any danger.

The elephants in a herd can form strong relationships that last for many years.

Females in charge

Herds are made up of female elephants, called cows, which are all related. The oldest female is the herd leader and is called the **matriarch**. She teaches her daughters and sisters where to find food and water over a large area. Male elephants leave the herd when they become adults and then either live alone or join small, temporary herds with other males.

These elephants are taking part in an experiment that tests how well they can work together.

HOW DO WE KNOW?

Scientists have studied Asian elephants in Thailand to see how well they can work as a team. Two elephants in an experiment were able to get to food treats if they pulled ropes at the same time. The elephants learned that if only one of them pulled a rope, they would not get a treat. The elephants quickly learned that they needed their partner to get a snack!

Elephant childcare

Another way an elephant herd works as a team is in caring for their young. Baby elephants are called calves. They drink their mother's milk, but other females in the herd will often also feed a calf that is hungry.

Mother elephants and their calves are almost always touching each other so that the mother can help and protect her baby, and a strong **bond** is formed.

The elephants in a herd will gather round the smallest calves to protect them when a **predator** is close.

Young female elephants that haven't yet had calves will help the mothers in a herd care for their babies. They will watch them and help them up hills and over rough ground as the herd travels. This practice gives the young females the knowledge they will need to care for their own calves when they are old enough.

CALF CARE

Elephants are pregnant for longer than any other mammal. Their **gestation period** lasts for 18 to 22 months. Mother elephants look after their calves for a very long time, much longer than many other mammals.

Elephant talk

Elephants' eyesight is not very strong, so they use their other senses to keep in touch with each other. Elephants within a herd touch each other with their trunks to communicate. This might be a gentle stroke if a calf is scared. Elephants greeting each other might intertwine their trunks and grip each other, a bit like shaking hands.

Elephants often raise their trunks when they sense danger. They trumpet when they feel fear or anger.

Elephant calls

African elephants can make around 25 different calls, each with its own meaning. These calls can be loud trumpets or roars, or quieter rumbles or snorts. Elephants can travel over long distances, so the rumbling sounds they make are very important. Scientists working in Namibia in Africa have discovered that elephants can hear deep rumblings from family members over at least 285 square kilometres (110 square miles)!

An elephant's sensitive trunk will feel vibrations in the ground that give it information about its surroundings.

HOW DO WE KNOW?

Scientist Caitlin O'Connell-Rodwell has studied elephant communication for many years. She carried out experiments with different types of sound recording to show how elephants feel **low-frequency** rumblings that travel through the ground. The vibrations travel through the elephants' bones, but she also discovered that elephants place their trunks on the ground to feel the calls more clearly.

Elephant emotions

Another way that elephants show their intelligence is through the way they become attached to each other. Elephants can show many different emotions and feelings towards each other, such as happiness when they are reunited with a family member or grief when a herd member dies.

The cows in a herd often show great happiness when a new calf is born. They make loud trumpeting noises, much like humans might cheer with excitement.

Fluid that comes out of special **glands** on an elephant's face may show that the elephant is feeling something very strongly.

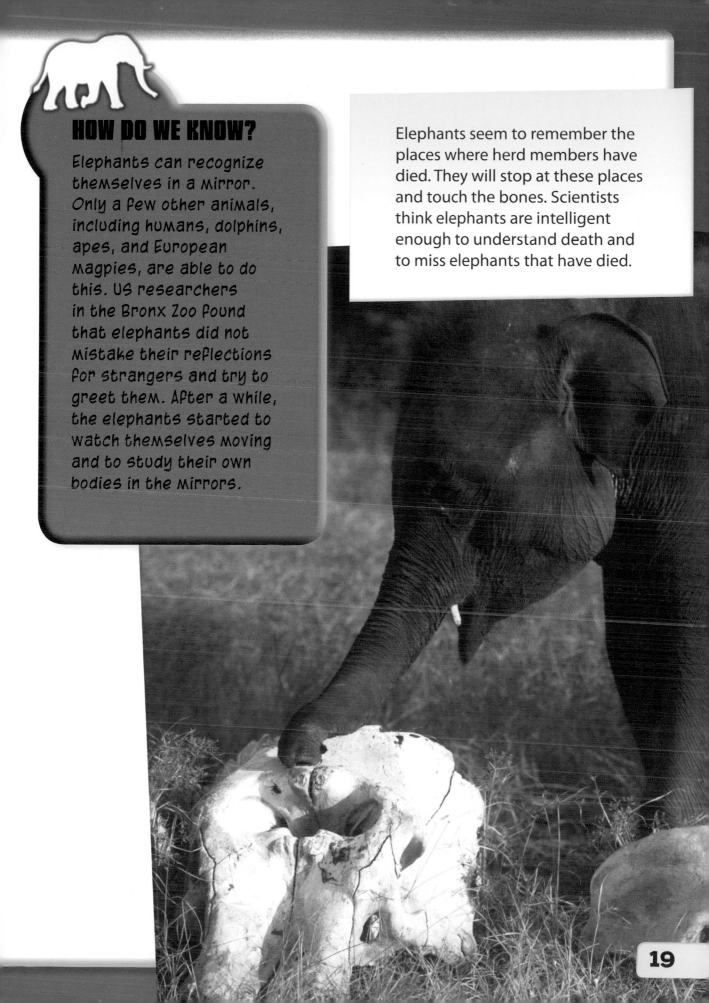

HOW DO WE KNOW?

Elephants can recognize themselves in a mirror. Only a few other animals, including humans, dolphins, apes, and European magpies, are able to do this. US researchers in the Bronx Zoo found that elephants did not mistake their reflections for strangers and try to greet them. After a while, the elephants started to watch themselves moving and to study their own bodies in the mirrors.

Elephants seem to remember the places where herd members have died. They will stop at these places and touch the bones. Scientists think elephants are intelligent enough to understand death and to miss elephants that have died.

Elephant memory

Elephants are well known for having incredible memories. As the oldest member of the herd, the matriarch needs to remember the way to a waterhole a long distance away when the herd needs water. She needs to pass this memory on through the herd so that when she dies, a new matriarch can take over and know where to go.

This is very important to the herd's survival. If the older members of a herd are killed, the whole herd could die because they can no longer find food or water.

In the dry season, it is very important for the herd to know where to find water so that they can survive.

Orphan elephants are cared for by human carers in projects such as this one in Kenya.

Remembering each other

Elephants remember each other over many years. They will recognize elephants who joined other herds, such as males that left their mother's herd when they became adults. Elephants will also remember humans who cared for them when they were calves many years after they have grown up and joined a wild herd.

Working with elephants

For hundreds of years, humans have trained Asian elephants to work for them. The elephants can be used to carry or drag heavy objects, especially in areas of forests where trees are cut down for their **timber**. In logging areas, elephants pull tree trunks that have been cut down to roads or rivers where the timber can be transported.

This elephant is moving logs in Thailand.

Elephants can still be found working on farmland or transporting supplies over rough ground. Asian elephants have also been used in ceremonies and processions, carrying important people on their backs.

FAST LEARNERS

Asian elephants can be trained by humans to remember instructions. Elephants learn quickly and can remember as many as 40 different commands from their trainer.

This Asian elephant is working on a beach in Vietnam.

People have not been able to train African elephants to work for humans in the same way as Asian elephants. However, a few elephants in tourist areas in Africa have been trained to carry people on their backs.

Protecting elephants

Today, Asian elephants are not used for work so widely because machinery has taken their place. Also, many people have **campaigned** against the use of elephants in logging because the work could be very hard and the animals were often treated badly.

However, in some places people are realizing that using elephants rather than machines is better for the environment. In north-east India, for example, people are using elephants to carry logs in order to avoid the destruction that logging machines can cause to their rainforest home. The elephants are treated well because they are so valuable.

Tourists love to see large animals, such as elephants, living in the wild.

ELEPHANTS IN DANGER

Elephants in Africa and Asia are in danger due to human activity. Some elephants are shot by **poachers** for their ivory tusks, while others are dying because they are losing much of their natural habitat to humans. Many people are working hard on **conservation** projects to protect these animals.

Tourism

Many tourists visiting Africa and Asia are keen to see elephants and learn about how they can be protected. In Asia, tourists are able to visit elephant **sanctuaries** and explore their natural environment. Some villages have developed projects where tourists can meet elephants and help to care for them, while also helping the local economy.

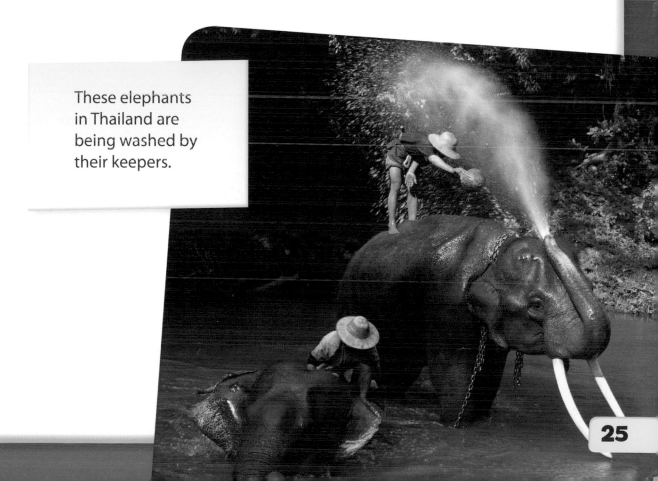

These elephants in Thailand are being washed by their keepers.

Copying elephants

Humans have tried to use technology to copy some of elephants' amazing abilities. Machines, such as diggers and bulldozers, are able to knock down trees and drag timber in place of elephants.

Elephants' strength and power are very useful, but their trunk is probably their most incredible tool. Engineers have tried to copy an elephant trunk by designing robotic arms that can reach up high and pick up tiny objects. German scientists invented the Bionic Handling Assistant, a very flexible robotic arm that can even sense when it is gripping part of a human so that it does not hurt them.

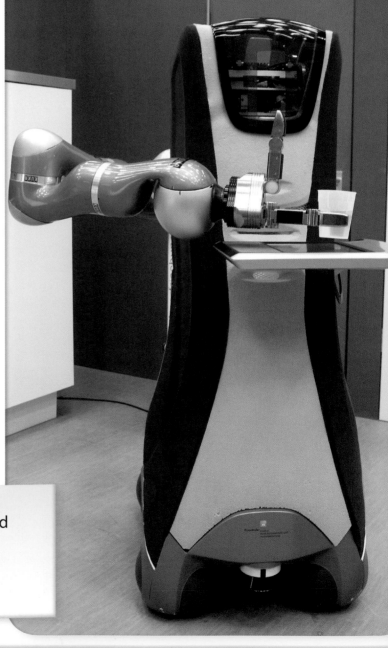

This robot is designed to pick things up and carry them like an elephant's trunk.

Early warning

Elephants' ability to hear low-frequency vibrations may also mean they can feel movement in the ground before an earthquake or tsunami. In 2004, a tsunami struck many coastlines around the Indian Ocean. Before the disaster happened, elephants in Thailand became stressed and moved to higher ground where they were safe. For hundreds of years, people have developed machines called seismographs to detect earthquakes the way that elephants do.

GOOD VIBRATIONS

This woman is having a hearing aid fitted. Researchers are investigating whether people like her can learn to hear low-frequency vibrations in a similar way to elephants, and use this to communicate.

The amazing elephant

Elephants really are wonderful animals with some surprising abilities. They can use tools, recognize themselves in the mirror, and care for each other in many different ways. They are huge and powerful creatures and don't have to fear any other animal – apart from humans. The biggest threat to elephants is people.

We need to do all we can to help protect these beautiful animals which we are still only beginning to understand.

Some Asian elephants have learned to hold a brush and paint pictures.

Elephant superpowers

If you could pick one of the amazing abilities elephants have, what would you choose?

- Would you have an incredible trunk, strong enough to move furniture around the house, but sensitive enough to pick up a single grape? Just think of the fun you'd have squirting water at your friends!

- Would you have huge ears you could flap to cool yourself down on a hot day?

- Would you learn to communicate with vibrations through the ground? You could talk to your friends in class without the teacher ever knowing!

- Would you choose to have an elephant's brilliant memory? Tests would never be a problem again!

Glossary

blood vessel long, thin tube that carries blood around the body

bond connection between people or animals with a close relationship

campaign take part in activities to spread a message or ask for change

conservation projects that work to protect natural environments

gestation period length of time an animal is pregnant

gland part of the body that produces a substance

habitat natural home for an animal or plant

low frequency made by very few sound waves and cannot be heard by a human ear

mammal type of warm-blooded animal that has a backbone, feeds on its mother's milk when young, and has hair on its body

matriarch oldest female in a herd who acts as leader

poacher person who kills animals illegally

predator animal that hunts and eats other animals

sanctuary (plural: sanctuaries) place where animals can be safe

savannah large grassland

social living together in groups

species particular type of living thing

timber trees that are cut down so the wood can be used

Find out more

Books

Elephant vs Rhinoceros (Animals Head to Head), Isabel Thomas (Raintree, 2007)

Elephants (Great Migrations), Laura Marsh (National Geographic, 2010)

Face to Face with Elephants, Beverly and Dereck Joubert (National Geographic, 2008)

Websites

www.bbc.co.uk/nature/life/Elephantidae
There are videos and lots of information about elephants on the BBC nature website.

gowild.wwf.org.uk/regions/africa-fact-files/african-elephant
gowild.wwf.org.uk/regions/asia-fact-files/sumatran-elephant
The WWF's website has fact files on different types of elephant.

kids.nationalgeographic.com/kids/animals/creaturefeature/african-elephant
The National Geographic website has information on many animals, including African elephants.

Places to visit

Chester Zoo, Caughall Road, Chester CH2 1LH
www.chesterzoo.org
To see a group of Asian elephants, visit Chester Zoo.

Whipsnade Zoo, Dunstable, Bedfordshire LU6 2LF
www.zsl.org/zsl-whipsnade-zoo
Visit the Asian elephants at the UK's largest zoo.

Index